Governing the United States

Ask the Governor

Christy Mihaly

Educational Media

rourkeeducationalmedia.com

BEFORE AND DURING READING ACTIVITIES

Before Reading: *Building Background Knowledge and Vocabulary*

Building background knowledge can help children process new information and build upon what they already know. Before reading a book, it is important to tap into what children already know about the topic. This will help them develop their vocabulary and increase their reading comprehension.

Questions and Activities to Build Background Knowledge:

1. Look at the front cover of the book and read the title. What do you think this book will be about?
2. What do you already know about this topic?
3. Take a book walk and skim the pages. Look at the table of contents, photographs, captions, and bold words. Did these text features give you any information or predictions about what you will read in this book?

Vocabulary: *Vocabulary Is Key to Reading Comprehension*

Use the following directions to prompt a conversation about each word.

- Read the vocabulary words.
- What comes to mind when you see each word?
- What do you think each word means?

Vocabulary Words:
- budget
- cabinet
- constitution
- departments
- executive
- legislature
- pardon
- veto

During Reading: *Reading for Meaning and Understanding*

To achieve deep comprehension of a book, children are encouraged to use close reading strategies. During reading, it is important to have children stop and make connections. These connections result in deeper analysis and understanding of a book.

Close Reading a Text

During reading, have children stop and talk about the following:

- Any confusing parts
- Any unknown words
- Text to text, text to self, text to world connections
- The main idea in each chapter or heading

Encourage children to use context clues to determine the meaning of any unknown words. These strategies will help children learn to analyze the text more thoroughly as they read.

When you are finished reading this book, turn to the next-to-last page for **Text-Dependent Questions** and an **Extension Activity**.

TABLE OF CONTENTS

What the Governor Does

The governor leads the state. How? Ask the governor!

What is the governor's job?

The governor runs the **executive** branch of one state in the United States. The executive branch carries out laws.

Governers discuss laws, meet with other officials, and talk about the state's problems. They work hard to make things better for citizens in their state.

How does someone become governor?

The state's voters elect the governor. The governor must be a state resident. They must be a United States citizen. Some states say they must be 35 years old. Other states have no age requirement.

The governor is usually elected for four years. Most states limit a governor to eight years. Then, someone else has a turn.

55 American Governors
Puerto Rico elects a governor. So do Guam, Northern Mariana Islands, U.S. Virgin Islands, and American Samoa. These are all U.S. territories or commonwealths. Together with a governor from each of the 50 states, that adds up to 55 American governors.

Who does the governor work with?

Governors work with their state's **legislature**. They work with mayors from cities in the state.

Most governors have a **cabinet**. This cabinet isn't for dishes! It's a group of people. Some cabinet members run government **departments**. They advise the governor.

The governor works with different departments in the state. The health department helps people in the state stay healthy. The parks department runs state parks. The people in these departments work for the governor.

What is the governor's day like?

Governors are busy. They make phone calls and go to meetings. They read important documents, write letters and emails, and post messages online. They want to keep in touch with the people.

First Woman
Nellie Tayloe Ross was governor of Wyoming. She was elected in 1924. Ross was America's first woman governor. She later directed the U.S. Mint for twenty years. The U.S. Mint makes coins.

Governors travel. They visit construction sites. They go to events. They tell people to come to their beautiful state!

Former South Carolina Governor Nikki Haley

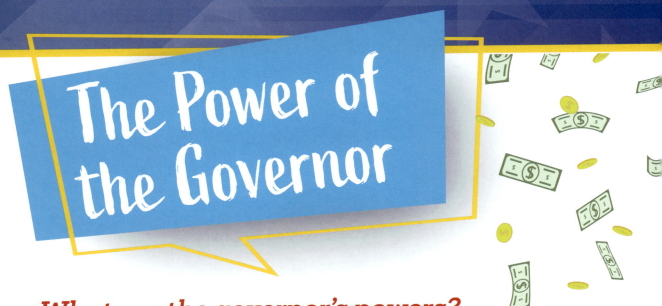

The Power of the Governor

What are the governor's powers?

The state **constitution** describes the governor's powers. The constitution is the state's highest law.

Most governors create a state **budget**. The budget plans how the state will get and spend money.

Governors cannot pass new laws. But they can **veto** laws. Governors hire people. They choose people for important state jobs. Many governors pick state judges.

Governors have a big role after disasters such as hurricanes. They can declare an emergency so state residents get help more quickly.

LIVE

BREAKING NEWS

BREAKING NEWS LIVE · BREAKING NEWS

24 LIVE NEWS

GOVERNOR SCOTT CALLS STATE OF EMERGENCY

What limits the governor's powers?

Judges can limit a governor's power. They decide if the governor's ideas and actions follow the law. Governors have lots of power, but they must obey the law.

The legislature can limit the governor's powers. It can reject the governor's budget. It can vote against the governor's ideas for new laws. Most legislatures can remove the governor from office if the governor breaks the law.

Voters have power too. They can limit the governor's powers by electing someone else. The governor cares what voters think.

What else do governors do?

Governors make speeches. They announce plans. They tell how they will fix problems. Sometimes, governors let prisoners go free. This is called a **pardon**.

Governors help people in trouble. They visit flooded homes. They go to burned places after fires. They send crews to clean up.

States Work Together
Governors can work together. The United States Climate Alliance started in 2017. Governors of different states formed this group. They wanted to fight climate change together. In 2019, the 25th state joined.

Governors do fun things too! They cut ribbons to open new buildings. They sign new laws. They give out awards.

Kim Reynolds
43rd Governor of Iowa

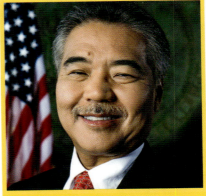

David Ige
8th Governor of Hawaii

Deval Patrick
71st Governor of Massachusetts

Susana Martinez
31st Governor of New Mexico

What state do you live in? Who is your governor?

Interesting Things About Being Governor

Do governors get special benefits?

Some governors live in a governor's mansion. This fancy house is owned by the state. It usually has rooms for public events.

Some governors get a state car. Many have drivers. The driver may be a state police officer.

Kid Candidates

In 2018, six Kansas high school students ran for governor. The teens lost. They were still glad they ran. They said more voters came out because they were running.

Look around your state. Is there something you would like to change? Why not tell your governor about it?

Government of the United States

Governors work in the executive branch of government. Can you find the governor in the chart?

	Legislative Branch Makes the laws.	**Executive Branch** Carries out the laws.	**Judicial Branch** Decides what laws mean.
Federal Governs the whole country.	**Congress** Includes Senators and members of the House of Representatives.	**The President** Works with cabinet members such as the Attorney General.	**U.S. Courts** Judges work at many courts, including the U.S. Supreme Court.
State Governs each of the 50 states.	**State Legislature** Representatives work at the capitol building in each state's capital city.	**The Governor** Works with many officials such as the Secretary of State.	**State Courts** Include the highest court in the state— the state Supreme Court.
Local Governs each village, town, or city.	**City Council** Representatives make rules about how land is used, where roads will be built, and more.	**The City Mayor** Is in charge of the police department, the parks department, and more.	**Local Courts** Judges rule on cases that involve city laws and crimes that are less serious.

Glossary

budget (BUHJ-it): a plan for how much money will come in and how it will be spent within a certain time

cabinet (KAB-uh-nit): a group of advisers for the head of a government

constitution (kahn-sti-TOO-shuhn): the basic laws of a country or state, setting out the powers of government and the rights of the people

departments (di-PAHRT-muhnts): sections of a larger organization that have a certain function or purpose, as in the tax department of a government

executive (ig-ZEK-yuh-tiv): relating to the branch of government that carries out the laws

legislature (LEJ-is-lay-chur): the group of people in a government with the power to make and change the laws

pardon (PAHR-duhn): forgiveness for a fault or offense

veto (VEE-toh): to stop a law that has been passed so it does not go into effect

Index

Text-Dependent Questions

1. What does a state budget do?
2. What are some ways the governor can help their state?
3. What are some limits on the governor's power?
4. What are some differences between the governor's powers and the legislature's powers?
5. Would you like to run for governor? Why or why not?

Extension Activity

Look up your governor's name and address on a state website or in a directory. Or ask a librarian, teacher, or other adult. Write a letter to the governor. Give your opinion about something they have done. Or tell them about a problem you see or an idea you have to improve life in your state.

ABOUT THE AUTHOR

Christy Mihaly has met the governors of two states, and she's pretty sure they're regular people. Christy has degrees in policy studies and law. She is the author of many books for young readers, including *Free for You and Me*, a picture book about the First Amendment to the United States Constitution. Find out more or say hello at her website: www.christymihaly.com.

www.rourkeeducationalmedia.com

PHOTO CREDITS: cover: ©jmoor17; page 4: ©penfold; page 5: © FEMA/Eduardo Martínez; page 6: ©FLAGOV; page 7: ©SDI Productions; pages 8-9: ©metamorworks; page 8: Wiki (inset); page 9: ©Rob Davis (inset); page 10: ©Zhenyakot; page 11: ©MikeMareen; page 12: ©sirtravelalot; page 13: ©gustavofrazao; page 14: ©Steve Debenport; page 15: ©Anne Belden, ©piyaset (inset); page 16: ©fac8ef_o; page 17: Public Domain; page 18: ©Jackie Wright; page 19: ©Nagel Photography; page 20: ©RichVintage

Edited by: Madison Capitano
Cover by: Rhea Magaro-Wallace
Interior design by: Janine Fisher

Library of Congress PCN Data

Ask the Governor / Christy Mihaly (Governing the United States)
ISBN 978-1-73162-905-0 (hard cover)
ISBN 978-1-73162-904-3 (soft cover)
ISBN 978-1-73162-906-7 (e-Book)
ISBN 978-1-73163-347-7 (ePub)
Library of Congress Control Number: 2019944971

Rourke Educational Media
Printed in the United States of America,
North Mankato, Minnesota